Bridgend Education Centre

KU-033-702

Intermediate 2 | Units 1, 2 & Applications

Mathematics

"2000" Specimen Question Paper
Paper 1 (Non-calculator)
Paper 2

Additional Specimen Question Paper
Paper 1 (Non-calculator)
Paper 2

2001 Exam
Paper 1 (Non-calculator)
Paper 2

2002 Exam
Paper 1 (Non-calculator)
Paper 2

2002 Winter Diet
Paper 1 (Non-calculator)
Paper 2

2003 Exam
Paper 1 (Non-calculator)
Paper 2

© Scottish Qualifications Authority

All rights reserved. Copying prohibited. No part of this publication may be reproduced, stored in a retrieval system, or transmitted in any form or by any means, electronic, mechanical, photocopying, recording or otherwise.

First exam published in 2000.
Published by
Leckie & Leckie, 8 Whitehill Terrace, St. Andrews, Scotland KY16 8RN
tel: 01334 475656 fax: 01334 477392
enquiries@leckieandleckie.co.uk www.leckieandleckie.co.uk

Leckie & Leckie Project Team: Peter Dennis; John MacPherson; Bruce Ryan; Andrea Smith

ISBN 1-84372-116-3

A CIP Catalogue record for this book is available from the British Library.

Printed in Scotland by Scotprint.

Leckie & Leckie is a division of Granada Learning Limited, part of Granada plc.

Scotland's leading educational publishers

Introduction

Dear Student,

This past paper book provides you with the perfect opportunity to put into practice everything you need to know in order to excel in your exams. The range of past papers offers you an invaluable insight into what to expect on the day and will help you to prepare thoroughly for your own exam this summer.

Work carefully through each past paper: the questions are designed to assess not only your subject knowledge and understanding, but also your ability to apply examinable skills developed throughout your course. By referring to the answer booklet at the back of the book you will understand exactly what the examiner is looking for to gain a top mark and will be able to focus on and improve in particular areas of your course which you find difficult. Remember too to use the top tips for revision and sitting the exam to make sure you perform to the best of your ability.

Practice makes perfect. Use these past papers to make sure you know what to expect on the day and are ready to succeed.

Good luck!

Acknowledgements

Every effort has been made to trace the copyright holders and to obtain their permission for the use of copyright material. Leckie & Leckie will gladly receive information enabling them to rectify any error or omission in subsequent editions.

[CO56/SQP201]

NATIONAL
QUALIFICATIONS

Time: 45 minutes

Specimen Question Paper
(based on the 2000 Question Paper)

MATHEMATICS
INTERMEDIATE 2
Units 1, 2 and
Applications of Mathematics
Paper 1
(Non-calculator)

Read carefully

1 **You may NOT use a calculator.**

2 Full credit will be given only where the solution contains appropriate working.

3 Square-ruled paper is provided.

SCOTTISH
QUALIFICATIONS
AUTHORITY

©

FORMULAE LIST

Sine rule: $\dfrac{a}{\sin A} = \dfrac{b}{\sin B} = \dfrac{c}{\sin C}$

Cosine rule: $a^2 = b^2 + c^2 - 2bc \cos A$ or $\cos A = \dfrac{b^2 + c^2 - a^2}{2bc}$

Area of a triangle: $\text{Area} = \frac{1}{2}ab \sin C$

Volume of a sphere: $\text{Volume} = \dfrac{4}{3}\pi r^3$

Volume of a cone: $\text{Volume} = \dfrac{1}{3}\pi r^2 h$

Volume of a cylinder: $\text{Volume} = \pi r^2 h$

Standard deviation: $s = \sqrt{\dfrac{\sum(x - \bar{x})^2}{n - 1}} = \sqrt{\dfrac{\sum x^2 - (\sum x)^2/n}{n - 1}}$, where n is the sample size.

Marks

1. A group of students scored the following marks in a test.

  9   5   6   8   6   9   7   8   6   5

   (*a*) Construct a frequency table from the above data and add a cumulative frequency column.   **2**

   (*b*) What is the probability that a student chosen at random from this group scored less than 8?   **1**

2.

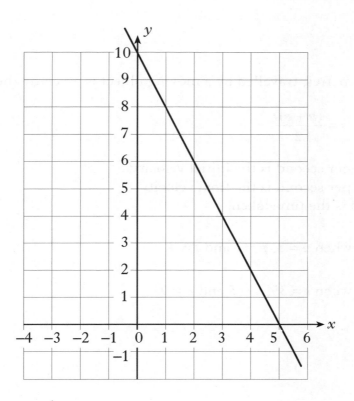

Find the equation of the straight line.   **3**

[Turn over

Marks

3. Stephen plans to go to a concert. The ticket costs £49·00. He works 2 hours overtime on Friday night at time and a half, and $2\frac{1}{2}$ hours overtime on Saturday morning at double time.

   If his basic pay is £6·80 per hour, will his overtime pay cover the cost of the ticket?

   You must give a reason for your answer.

   4

4. Factorise

   $$9a^2 - 25b^2.$$

   2

5. The distance, s metres, travelled by a moving object is given by the formula

   $$s = \frac{(u + v)t}{2}$$

   where u metres per second is the initial velocity,
   v metres per second is the final velocity
   and t seconds is the time taken.

   (a) Calculate s when $u = 3$, $v = 7$ and $t = 4$.

   3

   (b) Calculate t when $s = 35$, $u = 5$ and $v = 9$.

   3

Marks

6.

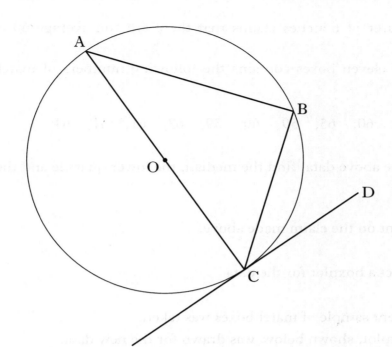

- A, B and C are points on the circumference of a circle, centre O.
- CD is a tangent to the circle.
- Angle BCD = 25°.

Calculate the size of angle BAC.

Show all working.

3

[Turn over for Question 7 on *Page six*

Marks

7. A manufacturer of matches claims that there are "on average 60 matches per box".

   A sample of eleven boxes contains the following numbers of matches per box.

   58, 62, 60, 65, 59, 60, 59, 62, 61, 61, 64

   (a) From the above data, find the median, the lower quartile and the upper quartile. **2**

   (b) Comment on the claim made above. **1**

   (c) Construct a boxplot for the data. **2**

   (d) A different sample of matchboxes was taken.
   The boxplot, shown below, was drawn for the new data.

   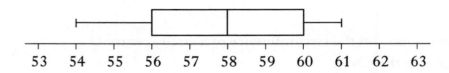

   Does this new data support the manufacturer's claim?
   Give a reason for your answer. **1**

[END OF QUESTION PAPER]

[CO56/SQP201]

NATIONAL
QUALIFICATIONS

Time: 1 hour 30 minutes

Specimen Question Paper
(based on the 2000 Question Paper)

MATHEMATICS
INTERMEDIATE 2
Units 1, 2 and
Applications of
Mathematics
Paper 2

Read carefully

1 **Calculators may be used in this paper.**

2 Full credit will be given only where the solution contains appropriate working.

3 Square-ruled paper is provided.

SCOTTISH
QUALIFICATIONS
AUTHORITY

©

FORMULAE LIST

Sine rule: $\dfrac{a}{\sin A} = \dfrac{b}{\sin B} = \dfrac{c}{\sin C}$

Cosine rule: $a^2 = b^2 + c^2 - 2bc\cos A$ or $\cos A = \dfrac{b^2 + c^2 - a^2}{2bc}$

Area of a triangle: Area $= \frac{1}{2}ab\sin C$

Volume of a sphere: Volume $= \dfrac{4}{3}\pi r^3$

Volume of a cone: Volume $= \dfrac{1}{3}\pi r^2 h$

Volume of a cylinder: Volume $= \pi r^2 h$

Standard deviation: $s = \sqrt{\dfrac{\sum (x - \bar{x})^2}{n-1}} = \sqrt{\dfrac{\sum x^2 - (\sum x)^2 / n}{n-1}}$, where n is the sample size.

Marks

1. A hotel inspector recorded the volume of wine, in millilitres, in a sample of six glasses.

   120   126   125   131   130   124

   Use an appropriate formula to calculate the standard deviation.
   Show clearly all your working.

   4

2. Multiply out the brackets and collect like terms.

   $$(3x + 2)(x - 1) + 4x$$

   3

3. The diagram shows a fold-away table whose top is in the shape of part of a circle.

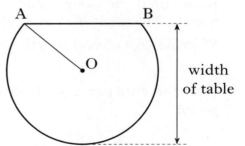

   • The centre of the circle is O.
   • AB is a chord of the circle.
   • AB is 70 centimetres.
   • The radius, OA, is 40 centimetres.

   Find the width of the table.

   4

[Turn over

Marks

4. Michael wishes to borrow £1000 for 3 months. He can choose from **Advantage Loans** or **Low Cost Loans**.

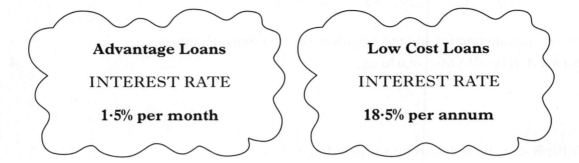

Advantage Loans	Low Cost Loans
INTEREST RATE	INTEREST RATE
1·5% per month	**18·5% per annum**

Which company costs less?
Give a reason for your answer.　　　　　　　　　　　　　　　　　　**4**

5. The cost of hiring a car depends on the number of days the car is hired and the number of litres of petrol used.

   (*a*) David hired a car for 3 days and used 50 litres of petrol. The total cost was £88·50.

      Let x pounds be the cost per day of hiring a car, and y pounds be the cost of one litre of petrol.

      Write down an equation in x and y which satisfies the above condition.　　**1**

   (*b*) Anne hired the same model of car for 4 days and used 60 litres of petrol. The total cost was £113·00.

      Write down a second equation in x and y which satisfies this condition.　　**1**

   (*c*) Find the cost per day of hiring the car and the cost of one litre of petrol.　　**4**

Marks

6. The flowchart below shows how to calculate the cost of joining a sports club.

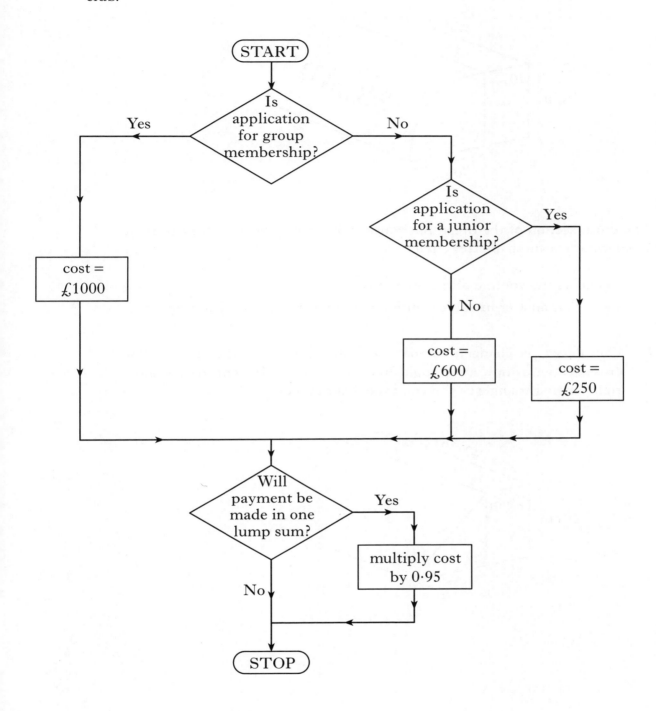

Use the flowchart to calculate the cost for an adult who wants to make the payment in one lump sum.

4

[Turn over

Marks

7. A bread bin is in the shape of a prism as shown below.

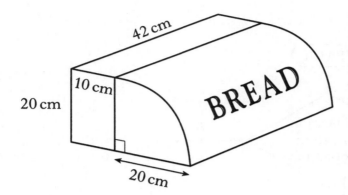

The cross-section of the bread bin consists of a rectangle 20 centimetres by 10 centimetres and a quarter circle.

(a) Calculate the volume of the bread bin.

Give your answer in cubic centimetres, correct to 3 significant figures. **4**

(b) The design is changed so that the volume remains the same. The cross-section is now a rectangle 20 centimetres by 10 centimetres and a right-angled triangle as shown in the diagram below.

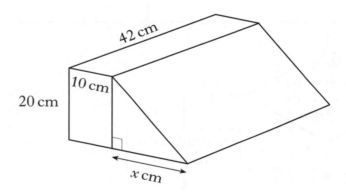

Find x. **3**

Marks

8.

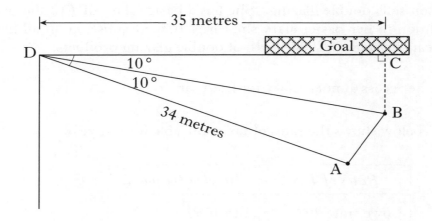

The diagram shows part of a football pitch with players at A, B, C and D.

BC is perpendicular to CD.

CD = 35 metres, angle CDB = 10°, angle BDA = 10°, AD = 34 metres.

Find the distance from A to B.   **5**

[Turn over

Marks

9. Lorna Simpson sells double glazing. She has a basic salary of £12 500 per year. In addition to her basic salary she earns 10% commission on all her sales. Last year she sold £50 000 worth of double glazing products.

   (a) Calculate her gross annual salary for last year.   2

   (b) The table below shows the rates of tax applicable for last year.

Rates of Tax	Taxable Income £
Lower rate 20%	1 to 4300
Basic rate 23%	4301 to 27 100
Higher rate 40%	over 27 100

   Lorna's total tax allowance is £4195.
   Calculate her annual tax bill for last year.   5

10. A survey was carried out to find the waiting time for telephone calls to be answered at a call centre. The results are shown below.

Time in seconds	Number of calls
20 − 34	9
35 − 49	10
50 − 64	14
65 − 79	19
80 − 94	22
95 −109	35
110 −124	21
125 −139	20

   Calculate the mean waiting time in seconds.   5

Marks

11. Heart-shaped cards have been designed for St Valentine's Day.

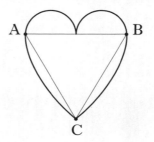

The template used is shown opposite with the key points A, B and C indicated.

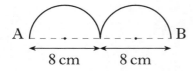

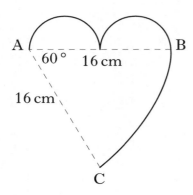

The top of the template was formed by drawing two semi-circles, each with diameter 8 centimetres.

One side of the template was formed by drawing an arc BC of a circle centre A, where angle BAC = 60°.

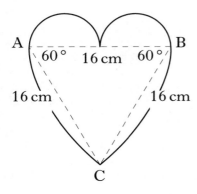

The template was completed by drawing arc AC of a circle centre B, where angle ABC = 60°.

Find the perimeter of the template. **5**

[END OF QUESTION PAPER]

[BLANK PAGE]

X101/202

NATIONAL
QUALIFICATIONS

Time: 1 hour 30 minutes

MATHEMATICS
INTERMEDIATE 2
Units 1, 2 and
Applications of Mathematics
Paper 1
(Non-calculator)

ADDITIONAL SPECIMEN QUESTION PAPER

Read carefully

1 **You may <u>NOT</u> use a calculator.**

2 Full credit will be given only where the solution contains appropriate working.

3 Square-ruled paper is provided.

SCOTTISH
QUALIFICATIONS
AUTHORITY

©

FORMULAE LIST

Sine rule: $\dfrac{a}{\sin A} = \dfrac{b}{\sin B} = \dfrac{c}{\sin C}$

Cosine rule: $a^2 = b^2 + c^2 - 2bc \cos A$ or $\cos A = \dfrac{b^2 + c^2 - a^2}{2bc}$

Area of a triangle: $\text{Area} = \dfrac{1}{2}ab \sin C$

Volume of a sphere: $\text{Volume} = \dfrac{4}{3}\pi r^3$

Volume of a cone: $\text{Volume} = \dfrac{1}{3}\pi r^2 h$

Volume of a cylinder: $\text{Volume} = \pi r^2 h$

Standard deviation: $s = \sqrt{\dfrac{\sum(x - \bar{x})^2}{n-1}} = \sqrt{\dfrac{\sum x^2 - (\sum x)^2 / n}{n-1}}$, where n is the sample size.

ALL questions should be attempted.

Marks

1.

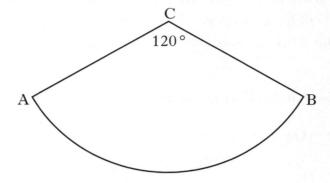

The diagram shows a sector of a circle, centre C and radius 15 centimetres.

AC and BC are radii.

Angle ACB is 120°.

Calculate the length of the arc AB.
(Take π = 3·14)

3

2.

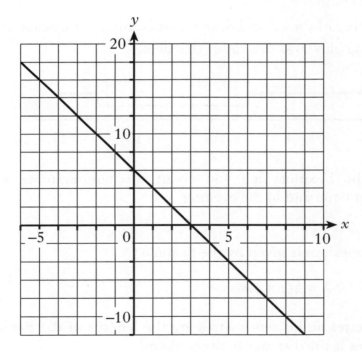

Find the equation of the straight line shown in the diagram.

3

Marks

3. Peter earns £6·50 per hour for a 36 hour week.

   For any extra hours worked he gets paid an overtime rate at time and a half.

   His deductions are 20% of his gross pay.

   Calculate his net pay for 41 hours worked.   **4**

4. Multiply out the brackets and collect like terms.

   $$5x\,(2x - 1) - x\,(x - 3)$$ **3**

5. The noon temperatures, in degrees Celsius, were recorded on the first day of June across the regions in the United Kingdom.

   The results are shown below.

   $$
   \begin{array}{ccccccccc}
   14 & 13 & 16 & 16 & 16 & 15 & 14 & 15 & 14 \\
   16 & 17 & 16 & 17 & 18 & 16 & 15 & 19 &
   \end{array}
   $$

   (*a*) From the results, find the median, the lower quartile and the upper quartile.   **3**

   (*b*) Construct a boxplot for the data.   **2**

   (*c*) On the evening of the same day, the temperatures were again recorded. The boxplot below was drawn for this data.

   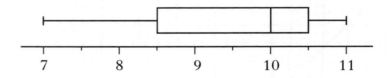

   What do the boxplots tell you about the temperatures and their variability at noon and in the evening?   **2**

6. The area of a trapezium is given by the formula

   $$A = \tfrac{1}{2}(p + q)h$$

   where *p* centimetres and *q* centimetres are the lengths of the parallel sides and *h* centimetres is the distance between them.

   (*a*) Calculate A when

   $p = 25{\cdot}2$, $q = 30{\cdot}5$ and $h = 24$.   **3**

   (*b*) Calculate *p* when

   $A = 615$, $q = 18{\cdot}6$ and $h = 30$.   **3**

   [END OF QUESTION PAPER]

X101/204

NATIONAL
QUALIFICATIONS

Time: 1 hour 30 minutes

MATHEMATICS
INTERMEDIATE 2
Units 1, 2 and
Applications of Mathematics
Paper 2

ADDITIONAL SPECIMEN QUESTION PAPER

Read carefully

1 **Calculators may be used in this paper.**

2 Full credit will be given only where the solution contains appropriate working.

3 Square-ruled paper is provided.

SCOTTISH
QUALIFICATIONS
AUTHORITY
©

FORMULAE LIST

Sine rule: $\dfrac{a}{\sin A} = \dfrac{b}{\sin B} = \dfrac{c}{\sin C}$

Cosine rule: $a^2 = b^2 + c^2 - 2bc \cos A$ or $\cos A = \dfrac{b^2 + c^2 - a^2}{2bc}$

Area of a triangle: $\text{Area} = \dfrac{1}{2}ab \sin C$

Volume of a sphere: $\text{Volume} = \dfrac{4}{3}\pi r^3$

Volume of a cone: $\text{Volume} = \dfrac{1}{3}\pi r^2 h$

Volume of a cylinder: $\text{Volume} = \pi r^2 h$

Standard deviation: $s = \sqrt{\dfrac{\sum(x - \bar{x})^2}{n-1}} = \sqrt{\dfrac{\sum x^2 - (\sum x)^2/n}{n-1}}$, where n is the sample size.

ALL questions should be attempted.

Marks

1. One hundred milligrams of an antibiotic are given to a patient.

   At the end of each hour the number of milligrams of antibiotic in the body is 20% less than at the beginning of that hour.

   How many milligrams of antibiotic remain in the body at the end of three hours?

   3

2.

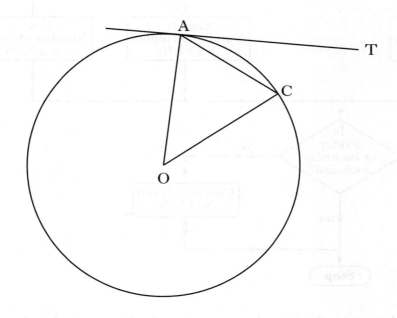

   AT is a tangent to the circle, centre O.

   Angle TAC is 26°.

   Calculate the size of angle AOC.

   3

3. Solve **algebraically** the system of equations

$$5x + 3y = 1$$
$$3x - 2y = 12.$$

   3

Marks

4. The flowchart below shows how to calculate the cost of a room in "The Castle Hotel".

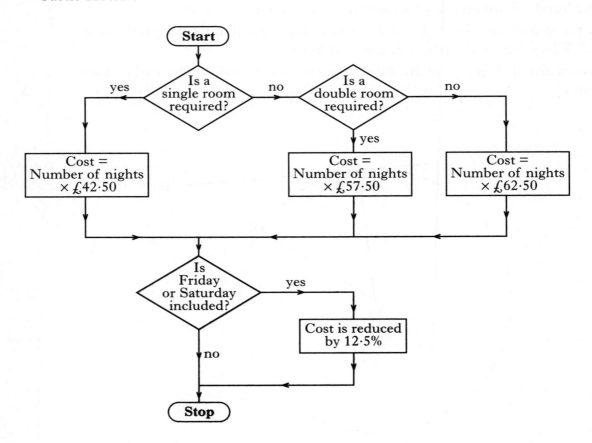

Use the flowchart to calculate the cost of a double room for 4 nights starting on Tuesday, 10 July.

4

5. A tutor asked students in his year group where they planned to go on holiday.

The responses are shown below.

Holiday	Frequency
UK	26
Europe (not UK)	63
USA	16
Others	15

Draw a piechart to illustrate this information.

4

Marks

6. The price, in pounds, of a meal in seven different restaurants is shown below.

   17   11   20   13   12   10   15

Use an appropriate formula to calculate the mean and standard deviation of these prices.

Show clearly all your working.   4

7. A triangular plot of ground, PRQ, is represented below.

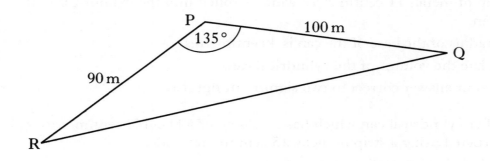

$PQ = 100$ metres, $PR = 90$ metres and angle $RPQ = 135°$.

Calculate the length of RQ.

Do not use a scale drawing.   4

8. Michael gets paid 0·5% commission on his total sales.

If his commission for May was £320, calculate his total sales for May.   2

Marks

9. (a)

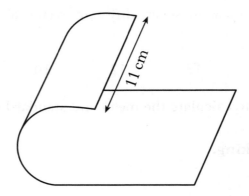

11 cm

A strip of metal, 11 centimetres wide, is rolled into the cylindrical wall of a can.

The radius of the base of the can is 4 centimetres.

Calculate the volume of the cylindrical can.

Give your answer correct to two significant figures. **3**

(b) Another cylindrical can which has a volume of 500 cubic centimetres is constructed using a strip of metal 15 centimetres wide.

Calculate the base radius of this can. **3**

10. Alex is going to take a loan to buy a new car.

MONTHLY REPAYMENTS

Amount borrowed	APR	60 months		48 months		24 months	
		NPP	WPP	NPP	WPP	NPP	WPP
£15 000	8·2%	307·85	314·01	370·73	378·14	687·10	700·84
£10 000	8·8%	208·13	212·29	250·04	255·05	461·07	470·29
£5000	8·8%	104·07	106·15	125·02	127·52	230·53	235·14

NPP = **no** payment protection

WPP = **with** payment protection

(a) If Alex borrows £10 000 over 2 years **without** payment protection, what is the cost of the loan? **3**

(b) The salesman persuades Alex to spread the payments over 4 years and to include payment protection.

Calculate the **increase** in the cost of the loan with this repayment method. **3**

Marks

11. The diagram below shows the position of three towns E, B and F.

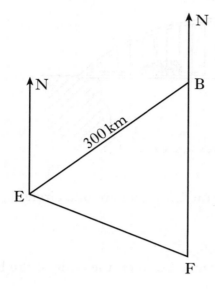

B is 300 kilometres from E.

From E, the bearing of B is 046°.

From E, the bearing of F is 116°.

F is due south of B.

How far apart are the towns E and F?

5

12. Information from a survey is analysed to find the time spent on an assignment by students.

The results are shown below.

Time (t minutes)	Frequency
$20 \leq t < 30$	3
$30 \leq t < 40$	7
$40 \leq t < 50$	12
$50 \leq t < 60$	15
$60 \leq t < 70$	10
$70 \leq t < 80$	3

(a) In which interval is the mode?

1

(b) Use a diagram to estimate the modal time taken.

3

Marks

13. The diagram below shows a road bridge.

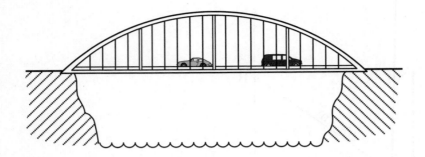

The curved part of the bridge is formed from an arc of a circle.

In the figure below,

- A represents the centre of the circle
- CD represents the horizontal distance between the ends of the bridge
- CD is 200 metres
- AC and AD are radii
- AC is 180 metres.

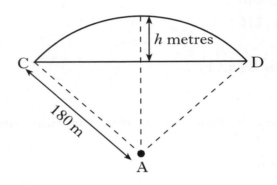

Find the height, *h* metres, of the bridge above its ends.   **4**

[END OF QUESTION PAPER]

INTERMEDIATE 2 2001

X056/202

NATIONAL
QUALIFICATIONS
2001

THURSDAY, 17 MAY
9.00 AM – 9.45 AM

MATHEMATICS
INTERMEDIATE 2
Units 1, 2 and
Applications of Mathematics
Paper 1
(Non-calculator)

Read carefully

1   **You may NOT use a calculator.**

2   Full credit will be given only where the solution contains appropriate working.

3   Square-ruled paper is provided.

SCOTTISH
QUALIFICATIONS
AUTHORITY
©

FORMULAE LIST

Sine rule: $\dfrac{a}{\sin A} = \dfrac{b}{\sin B} = \dfrac{c}{\sin C}$

Cosine rule: $a^2 = b^2 + c^2 - 2bc \cos A$ or $\cos A = \dfrac{b^2 + c^2 - a^2}{2bc}$

Area of a triangle: $\text{Area} = \frac{1}{2}ab \sin C$

Volume of a sphere: $\text{Volume} = \frac{4}{3}\pi r^3$

Volume of a cone: $\text{Volume} = \frac{1}{3}\pi r^2 h$

Volume of a cylinder: $\text{Volume} = \pi r^2 h$

Standard deviation: $s = \sqrt{\dfrac{\sum(x - \bar{x})^2}{n-1}} = \sqrt{\dfrac{\sum x^2 - (\sum x)^2 / n}{n-1}}$, where n is the sample size.

ALL questions should be attempted.

Marks

1. Factorise

    $x^2 + 2x - 15$.

    2

2.

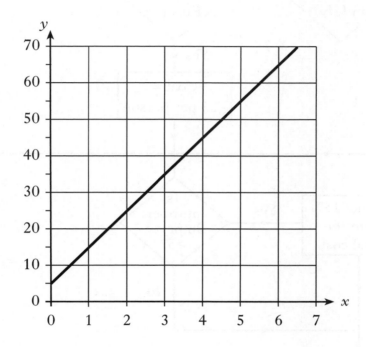

Find the equation of the straight line.

3

[Turn over

Marks

3. The flowchart below shows how to find the cost of travel insurance for a 17 day holiday.

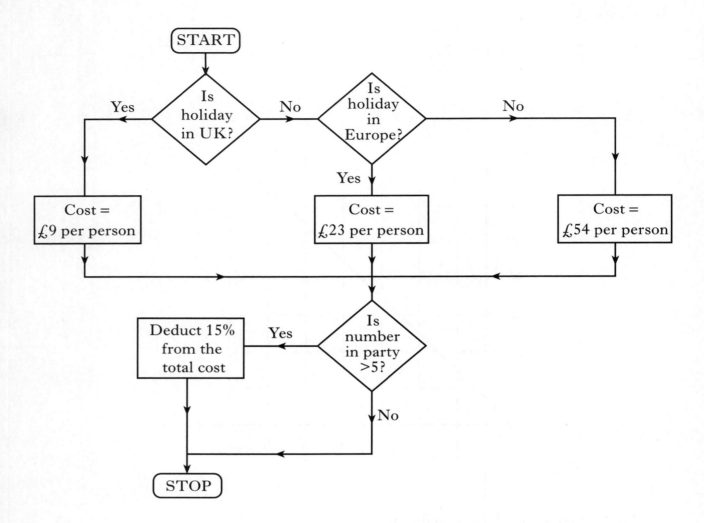

Use the flowchart to find the total insurance cost for a party of six planning a 17 day holiday to Europe.

4

4. Find the point of intersection of the straight lines with equations $2x + y = 5$ and $x - 3y = 6$.

4

Marks

5. The stem and leaf diagram shows the amounts of money spent by customers in a shop.

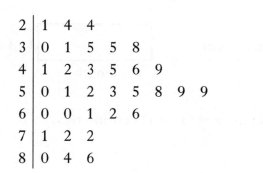

2	1 4 4
3	0 1 5 5 8
4	1 2 3 5 6 9
5	0 1 2 3 5 8 9 9
6	0 0 1 2 6
7	1 2 2
8	0 4 6

$n = 33$ $2|1$ represents 21 pence

(a) Using the above information, find
   (i) the median   **1**
   (ii) the lower quartile and the upper quartile   **2**
   (iii) the semi-interquartile range.   **2**

(b) What is the probability that a customer chosen at random spent more than 80 pence?   **1**

6. The area of the earring, shown below, is given by the formula

$$A = ac - \frac{3}{2}b^2.$$

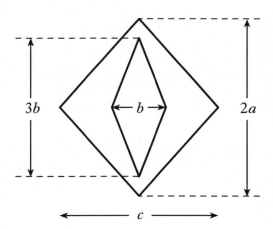

(a) Calculate A when $a = 25$, $b = 14$ and $c = 40$.   **2**

(b) Calculate b when $A = 550$, $a = 20$ and $c = 35$.   **4**

[Turn over

Marks

7. The square and rectangle shown below have the same **perimeter**.

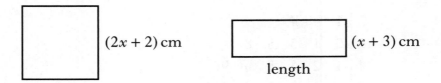

$(2x + 2)$ cm $(x + 3)$ cm

length

Show that the length of the rectangle is $(3x + 1)$ centimetres.   **2**

[*END OF QUESTION PAPER*]

X056/204

NATIONAL
QUALIFICATIONS
2001

THURSDAY, 17 MAY
10.05 AM – 11.35 AM

MATHEMATICS
INTERMEDIATE 2
Units 1, 2 and
Applications of Mathematics
Paper 2

Read carefully

1 **Calculators may be used in this paper.**

2 Full credit will be given only where the solution contains appropriate working.

3 Square-ruled paper is provided.

LIB X056/204 6/28870

SCOTTISH
QUALIFICATIONS
AUTHORITY

©

FORMULAE LIST

Sine rule: $\dfrac{a}{\sin A} = \dfrac{b}{\sin B} = \dfrac{c}{\sin C}$

Cosine rule: $a^2 = b^2 + c^2 - 2bc \cos A$ or $\cos A = \dfrac{b^2 + c^2 - a^2}{2bc}$

Area of a triangle: $\text{Area} = \frac{1}{2}ab \sin C$

Volume of a sphere: $\text{Volume} = \frac{4}{3}\pi r^3$

Volume of a cone: $\text{Volume} = \frac{1}{3}\pi r^2 h$

Volume of a cylinder: $\text{Volume} = \pi r^2 h$

Standard deviation: $s = \sqrt{\dfrac{\sum(x - \bar{x})^2}{n-1}} = \sqrt{\dfrac{\sum x^2 - (\sum x)^2 / n}{n-1}}$, where n is the sample size.

ALL questions should be attempted.

Marks

1. The population of a city is increasing at a steady rate of 2·4% per annum. The present population is 528 000.

   What is the expected population in 4 years time?

   Give your answer to the nearest thousand. **3**

2. Two groups of six students are given the same test.

   (a) The marks of Group A are

   $$73 \quad 47 \quad 59 \quad 71 \quad 48 \quad 62.$$

   Use an appropriate formula to calculate the mean and the standard deviation.

   Show clearly all your working. **4**

   (b) In Group B, the mean is 60 and the standard deviation is 29·8.

   Compare the results of the two groups. **2**

3. The contents of twenty matchboxes were counted.

   $$44 \quad 44 \quad 46 \quad 45 \quad 47 \quad 48 \quad 47 \quad 41 \quad 48 \quad 45$$
   $$45 \quad 44 \quad 42 \quad 43 \quad 44 \quad 46 \quad 46 \quad 43 \quad 49 \quad 45$$

   (a) Construct a dot plot for the data. **2**

   (b) Describe the shape of the distribution. **1**

   (c) What would you expect the "average contents per matchbox" to be ? **1**

   [Turn over

Marks

4. Gordon and Brian leave a hostel at the same time.

Gordon walks on a bearing of 045° at a speed of 4·4 kilometres per hour.

Brian walks on a bearing of 100° at a speed of 4·8 kilometres per hour.

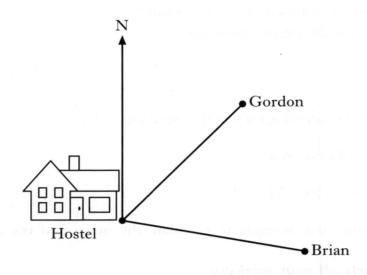

If they both walk at steady speeds, how far apart will they be after 2 hours?　　**5**

5. Anne Ibbotson works for a computer software company. Her March salary slip, shown below, is partly completed.

Name	Employee No.	N.I. No.	Tax Code	Month
A. Ibbotson	01987623	YT91875F	443L	March

Basic Salary	Commission	Overtime	Gross Salary
£2000		Nil	

Nat. Insurance	Income Tax	Pension	Total Deductions
£158·00	£421·21		

			Net Salary

(a) Anne is paid a basic monthly salary of £2000 plus commission of 12% of her total monthly sales.

Calculate her gross salary for March when her sales totalled £3398.　　**2**

(b) 6% of Anne's gross monthly salary is paid into her pension fund.

Calculate Anne's net salary for March.　　**3**

Mark

6. A drinks container is in the shape of a cylinder with radius 20 centimetres and height 50 centimetres.

   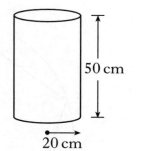

   (*a*) Calculate the volume of the drinks container.

   Give your answer in cubic centimetres, correct to two significant figures. **3**

   (*b*) Liquid from the full container can fill 800 cups, in the shape of cones, each of radius 3 centimetres.

   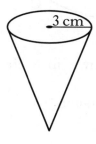

   What will be the height of liquid in each cup? **4**

7. Multiply out the brackets and collect like terms.

$$(x + 4)(2x^2 + 3x - 1)$$ **3**

[Turn over

Marks

8.

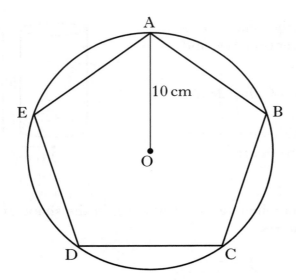

A regular pentagon ABCDE is drawn in a circle, centre O, with radius 10 centimetres.

Calculate the area of the regular pentagon.

5

9. The table below shows the monthly repayments to be made, with and without payment protection, when money is borrowed from the Cheaper Deals Loan Company.

	Amount	£1000	£2000	£3000	£4000
12 months	With Payment Protection	£101·40	£202·78	£304·42	£405·57
	Without Payment Protection	£88·17	£176·33	£264·50	£352·67
24 months	With Payment Protection	£53·48	£106·95	£160·43	£213·90
	Without Payment Protection	£46·50	£93·00	£139·50	£186·00
36 months	With Payment Protection	£37·51	£75·01	£112·51	£150·02
	Without Payment Protection	£32·61	£65·22	£97·84	£130·44

Sophina Iqbal wants to borrow £3000 to buy a conservatory and wants to make repayments over 24 months **with** payment protection.

(*a*) Calculate how much this loan will cost Sophina.

3

(*b*) How much would she save if she took out the same loan over 24 months **without** payment protection?

3

Marks

10. The diagram shows a mirror which has been designed for a new hotel.

    The shape consists of a sector of a circle and a kite AOCB.

    - The circle, centre O, has a radius of 50 centimetres.
    - Angle AOC = 140°.
    - AB and CB are tangents to the circle at A and C respectively.

    Find the perimeter of the mirror.

    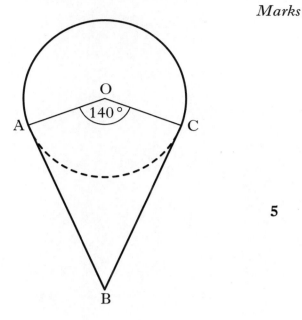

    5

11. Greenfingers Garden Centre keeps a record of the number of plants bought by each customer during one day. The results are shown below.

Number of plants	Frequency
1 – 10	25
11 – 20	46
21 – 30	55
31 – 40	49
41 – 50	36

    Calculate the mean number of plants bought by each customer.

    5

[END OF QUESTION PAPER]

[BLANK PAGE]

X101/202

NATIONAL
QUALIFICATIONS
2002

MONDAY, 27 MAY
1.00 PM – 1.45 PM

MATHEMATICS
INTERMEDIATE 2
Units 1, 2 and
Applications of Mathematics
Paper 1
(Non-calculator)

Read carefully

1 **You may NOT use a calculator.**

2 Full credit will be given only where the solution contains appropriate working.

3 Square-ruled paper is provided.

SCOTTISH
QUALIFICATIONS
AUTHORITY

FORMULAE LIST

Sine rule: $\dfrac{a}{\sin A} = \dfrac{b}{\sin B} = \dfrac{c}{\sin C}$

Cosine rule: $a^2 = b^2 + c^2 - 2bc \cos A$ or $\cos A = \dfrac{b^2 + c^2 - a^2}{2bc}$

Area of a triangle: $\text{Area} = \frac{1}{2}ab \sin C$

Volume of a sphere: $\text{Volume} = \frac{4}{3}\pi r^3$

Volume of a cone: $\text{Volume} = \frac{1}{3}\pi r^2 h$

Volume of a cylinder: $\text{Volume} = \pi r^2 h$

Standard deviation: $s = \sqrt{\dfrac{\sum(x - \bar{x})^2}{n-1}} = \sqrt{\dfrac{\sum x^2 - (\sum x)^2 / n}{n-1}}$, where n is the sample size.

ALL questions should be attempted.

Marks

1. In a tournament a group of golfers recorded the following scores.

    74 70 71 73 75 71 73 72

    72 75 71 76 74 72 70 73

    (a) Construct a frequency table from the above data and add a cumulative
         frequency column.   2

    (b) What is the probability that a golfer chosen at random from this group
         recorded a score of less than 72?   1

2. Suzy has a part-time job in a supermarket. Her basic rate of pay is £4·60
    per hour with rates of time and a half for work on Sundays and double time
    on Bank Holidays.

    If she works

    • Friday 3 hours
    • Saturday 7 hours
    • Sunday 2 hours
    • Bank Holiday Monday 6 hours

    calculate her gross pay.   4

3.

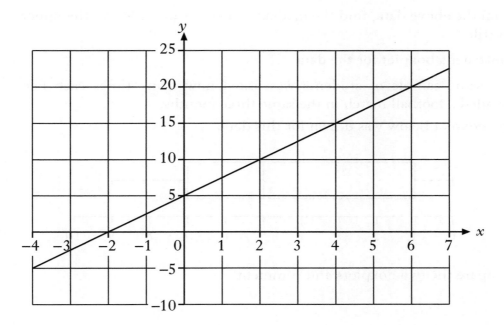

Find the equation of the straight line shown in the diagram.   3

[Turn over

Marks

4.

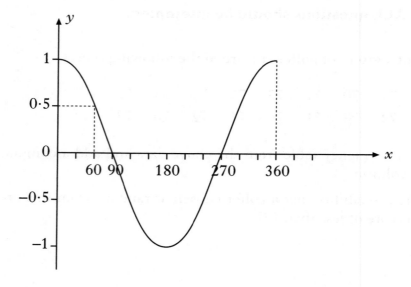

Part of the graph of $y = \cos x^\circ$ is shown above.

If $\cos 60^\circ = 0{\cdot}5$, state two values for x for which $\cos x^\circ = -0{\cdot}5$, $0 \le x \le 360$.   **2**

5. A sample of students was asked how many times each had visited the cinema in the last three months.

The results are shown below.

4	5	4	1	4	3	2	2	4	6	2
3	4	4	1	3	1	2	3	1	1	

(*a*) From the above data, find the median, the lower quartile and the upper quartile.   **3**

(*b*) Construct a boxplot for the data.   **2**

(*c*) The same sample of students was asked how many times each had attended a football match in the same three months.

The boxplot below was drawn for this data.

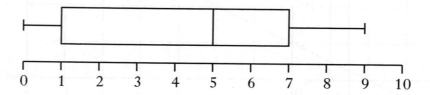

Compare the two boxplots and comment.   **1**

Marks

6. The surface area of the shape below is given by the formula

$$S = b(3l + h).$$

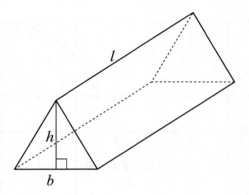

Find h when $S = 3340$, $b = 20$ and $l = 50$.   **3**

7. Multiply out the brackets and collect like terms.

$$(x - 3)(x^2 + 4x - 1)$$ **3**

[Turn over for Question 8 on *Page six*

Marks

8. A call centre records the duration, in seconds, of each of 80 phone calls. The results are shown in the cumulative frequency curve below.

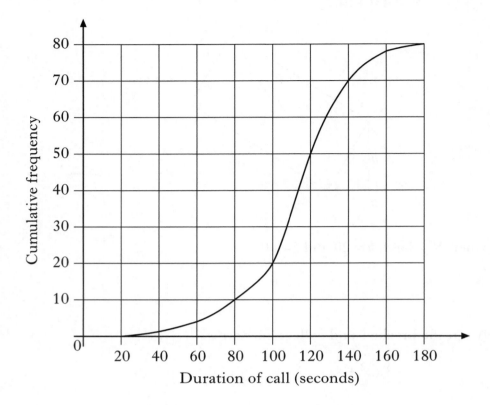

Duration of call (seconds)

(a) How many calls lasted 80 seconds or less?   1

(b) The call centre wishes to ensure that at least 75% of calls last no longer than 2 minutes. From the information given, has this been achieved?

Give a reason for your answer.   2

[END OF QUESTION PAPER]

X101/204

NATIONAL
QUALIFICATIONS
2002

MONDAY, 27 MAY
2.05 PM – 3.35 PM

MATHEMATICS
INTERMEDIATE 2
Units 1, 2 and
Applications of Mathematics
Paper 2

Read carefully

1 **Calculators may be used in this paper.**

2 Full credit will be given only where the solution contains appropriate working.

3 Square-ruled paper is provided.

SCOTTISH
QUALIFICATIONS
AUTHORITY

FORMULAE LIST

Sine rule: $\dfrac{a}{\sin A} = \dfrac{b}{\sin B} = \dfrac{c}{\sin C}$

Cosine rule: $a^2 = b^2 + c^2 - 2bc \cos A$ or $\cos A = \dfrac{b^2 + c^2 - a^2}{2bc}$

Area of a triangle: $\text{Area} = \dfrac{1}{2}ab \sin C$

Volume of a sphere: $\text{Volume} = \dfrac{4}{3}\pi r^3$

Volume of a cone: $\text{Volume} = \dfrac{1}{3}\pi r^2 h$

Volume of a cylinder: $\text{Volume} = \pi r^2 h$

Standard deviation: $s = \sqrt{\dfrac{\sum(x - \bar{x})^2}{n-1}} = \sqrt{\dfrac{\sum x^2 - (\sum x)^2/n}{n-1}}$, where n is the sample size.

ALL questions should be attempted.

Marks

1. The sketch shows a triangle, ABC.

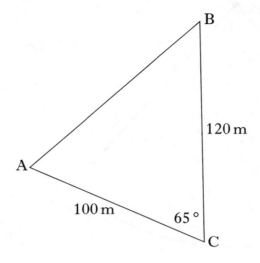

Calculate the area of the triangle.   **2**

2. Solve **algebraically** the system of equations

$$3x - 2y = 11$$
$$2x + 5y = 1.$$ **3**

3. (*a*) The price, in pence, of a carton of milk in six different supermarkets is shown below.

     66   70   89   75   79   59

Use an appropriate formula to calculate the mean and standard deviation of these prices.
Show clearly all your working.   **4**

(*b*) In six local shops, the mean price of a carton of milk is 73 pence with a standard deviation of 17·7.
Compare the supermarket prices with those of the local shops.   **2**

[Turn over

Marks

4. A pendulum travels along an arc of a circle, centre C.

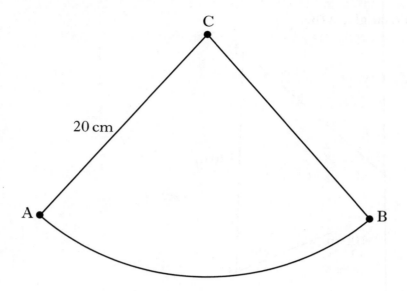

The length of the pendulum is 20 centimetres.

The pendulum swings from A to B.

The length of the arc AB is 28·6 centimetres.

Find the angle through which the pendulum swings from A to B.

4

5. (*a*) Factorise completely

$$3y^2 - 6y.$$

1

(*b*) Factorise

$$y^2 + y - 6.$$

2

Marks

6. A container to hold chocolates is in the shape of part of a cone with dimensions as shown below.

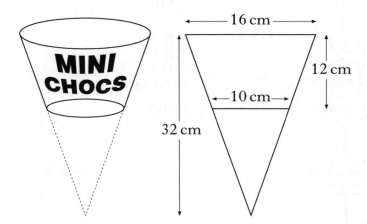

Calculate the volume of the container.

Give your answer correct to one significant figure.

5

[Turn over

Marks

7. The flowchart below shows how to calculate the interest when a certain amount of money is invested for 1 year.

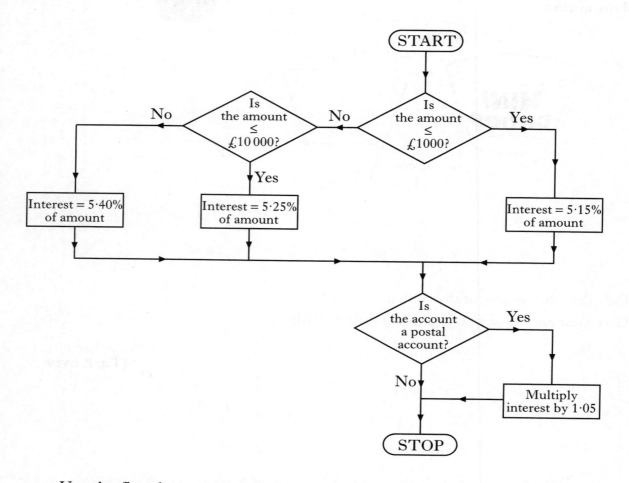

Use the flowchart to calculate the interest earned on an amount of £6000 invested in a postal account for 1 year.

4

Marks

8. The diagram shows two positions of a surveyor as he views the top of a flagpole.

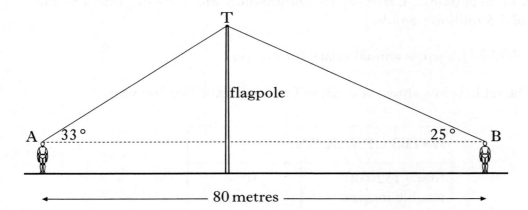

From position A, the angle of elevation to T at the top of the flagpole is 33°.

From position B, the angle of elevation to T at the top of the flagpole is 25°.

The distance AB is 80 metres and the height of the surveyor to eye level is 1·6 metres.

Find the height of the flagpole.

6

9. The population of Newtown is 50 000.

The population of Newtown is **increasing** at a steady rate of 5% per annum.

The population of Coaltown is 108 000.

The population of Coaltown is **decreasing** at a steady rate of 20% per annum.

How many years will it take until the population of Newtown is greater than the population of Coaltown?

5

[Turn over

Marks

10. Ian Smith is an engineer. His basic salary is £32 525 per year. In addition to his basic salary he receives a bonus of £1300 and earns commission on all orders he negotiates. Last year his commission was 0·2% on orders to the value of 1·5 million pounds.

(*a*) Calculate his gross annual salary for last year.   2

(*b*) The table below shows the rates of tax applicable for last year.

RATES OF TAX ON:	
first £1520 of taxable income	10%
next £26 880 of taxable income	22%
all remaining taxable income	40%

Ian's total tax allowance is £4385.

Calculate his annual tax bill for last year.   5

Marks

11. The diagram below shows a circular cross-section of a cylindrical oil tank.

In the figure below,

- O represents the centre of the circle
- PQ represents the surface of the oil in the tank
- PQ is 3 metres
- the radius OP is 2·5 metres.

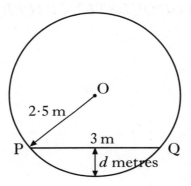

Find the depth, *d* metres, of oil in the tank.

4

[Turn over over for Question 12 on *Page ten*

Marks

12. Data from a recent census is analysed to find the age of residents in Crown Street.

    The results are shown below.

Age (to the nearest year)	Number of Residents
0 – 9	4
10 – 19	9
20 – 29	11
30 – 39	16
40 – 49	21
50 – 59	18
60 – 69	17
70 – 79	5

Calculate the mean age of the residents. **5**

[END OF QUESTION PAPER]

INTERMEDIATE 2

2002 WINTER DIET

W101/202

NATIONAL QUALIFICATIONS 2002	FRIDAY, 18 JANUARY 9.00 AM – 9.45 AM

MATHEMATICS
INTERMEDIATE 2
Units 1, 2 and
Applications of Mathematics
Paper 1
(Non-calculator)

Read carefully

1 **You may <u>NOT</u> use a calculator.**

2 Full credit will be given only where the solution contains appropriate working.

3 Square-ruled paper is provided.

SCOTTISH
QUALIFICATIONS
AUTHORITY

FORMULAE LIST

Sine rule: $\dfrac{a}{\sin A} = \dfrac{b}{\sin B} = \dfrac{c}{\sin C}$

Cosine rule: $a^2 = b^2 + c^2 - 2bc\cos A$ or $\cos A = \dfrac{b^2 + c^2 - a^2}{2bc}$

Area of a triangle: $\text{Area} = \dfrac{1}{2}ab\sin C$

Volume of a sphere: $\text{Volume} = \dfrac{4}{3}\pi r^3$

Volume of a cone: $\text{Volume} = \dfrac{1}{3}\pi r^2 h$

Volume of a cylinder: $\text{Volume} = \pi r^2 h$

Standard deviation: $s = \sqrt{\dfrac{\sum(x - \bar{x})^2}{n-1}} = \sqrt{\dfrac{\sum x^2 - (\sum x)^2/n}{n-1}}$, where n is the sample size.

ALL questions should be attempted.

Marks

1. The marks of a group of students in a class test and in the final exam are shown in the scattergraph below.

   A line of best fit has been drawn.

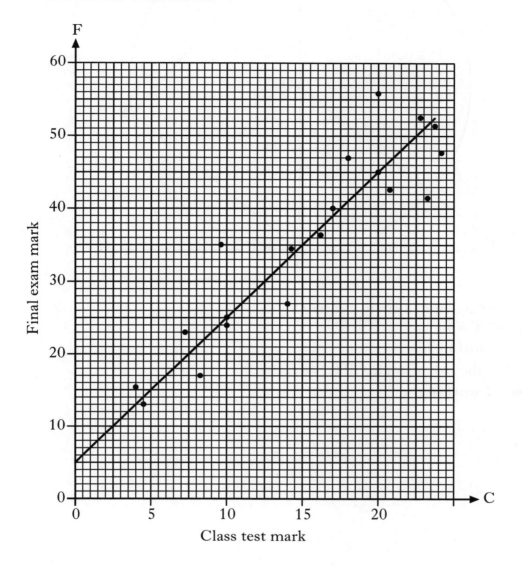

   (a) Find the equation of the line of best fit. 3

   (b) **Use your answer to part (a)** to predict the final exam mark for a student who achieved a mark of 12 in the class test. 1

[Turn over

Marks

2.

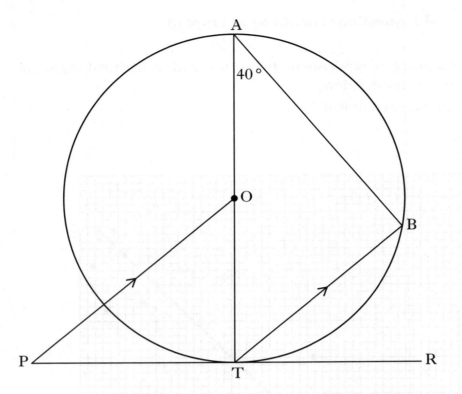

PTR is a tangent to a circle, centre O.

Angle BAT = 40°.

PO is parallel to TB.

Calculate the size of angle OPT.

Show all working.

3

Marks

3. The stem and leaf diagram shows the heights, to the nearest centimetre, of a group of female students.

$$
\begin{array}{c|cccccc}
14 & 8 \\
15 & 6 \\
16 & 0 & 4 & 8 & 9 \\
17 & 1 & 2 & 4 & 4 & 5 & 8 \\
18 & 8 \\
\end{array}
$$

$n = 13$ 14|8 represents 148 cm

(a) Using the above information, find

   (i) the median   **1**

   (ii) the lower quartile and the upper quartile.   **2**

(b) Draw a boxplot to illustrate this data.   **2**

(c) A sample of male students from the same course was taken. The heights, to the nearest centimetre, of these students were recorded.

The boxplot, shown below, illustrates this new data.

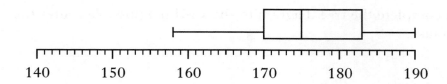

By comparing the boxplots, make **two** appropriate comments about the heights of the female and the male students.   **2**

[Turn over

Marks

4. The mileage chart shown below indicates how far it is between four places in Scotland.

Inverness

174

Glasgow

65	102

Fort William

106	149	157

Aberdeen

A lorry driver leaves Inverness and has to make deliveries to Glasgow, Fort William and Aberdeen. He cannot go through any place more than once and does not need to return to Inverness.

(a) Copy and complete the tree diagram to show **all** the possible routes the driver can take.

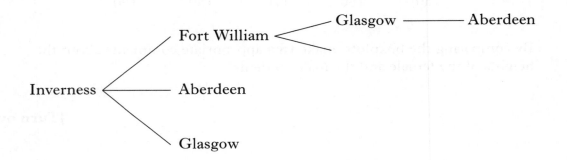

3

(b) He decides to take the route

Inverness — Fort William — Glasgow — Aberdeen.

What distance is this route?

1

Marks

5. The distance, S metres, travelled by an accelerating object is given by the formula

$$S = ut + \tfrac{1}{2}at^2$$

where u metres per second is the initial velocity,

    t seconds is the time taken

and a metres per second per second is the acceleration.

(*a*) Calculate S when $u = 30$, $t = 5$ and $a = 4$.   **3**

(*b*) Calculate u when $S = 294$, $t = 6$ and $a = 3$.   **3**

6.

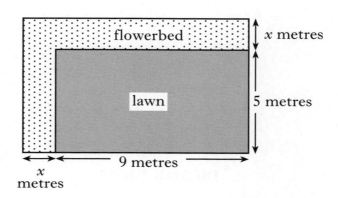

The diagram shows a rectangular garden which consists of a rectangular lawn and a flowerbed along two sides of the lawn

- the lawn measures 9 metres by 5 metres
- the width of the flowerbed is x metres.

(*a*) State the length and breadth of the garden.   **1**

(*b*) Show that the area, A square metres, of the garden is given by

$$A = x^2 + 14x + 45.$$ **2**

[END OF QUESTION PAPER]

[BLANK PAGE]

W101/204

NATIONAL
QUALIFICATIONS
2002

FRIDAY, 18 JANUARY
10.05 AM – 11.35 AM

MATHEMATICS
INTERMEDIATE 2
Units 1, 2 and
Applications of Mathematics
Paper 2

Read carefully

1 **Calculators may be used in this paper.**

2 Full credit will be given only where the solution contains appropriate working.

3 Square-ruled paper is provided.

LIB W101/204 6/530

SCOTTISH
QUALIFICATIONS
AUTHORITY

FORMULAE LIST

Sine rule: $\dfrac{a}{\sin A} = \dfrac{b}{\sin B} = \dfrac{c}{\sin C}$

Cosine rule: $a^2 = b^2 + c^2 - 2bc \cos A$ or $\cos A = \dfrac{b^2 + c^2 - a^2}{2bc}$

Area of a triangle: $\text{Area} = \frac{1}{2}ab \sin C$

Volume of a sphere: $\text{Volume} = \frac{4}{3}\pi r^3$

Volume of a cone: $\text{Volume} = \frac{1}{3}\pi r^2 h$

Volume of a cylinder: $\text{Volume} = \pi r^2 h$

Standard deviation: $s = \sqrt{\dfrac{\sum(x - \bar{x})^2}{n-1}} = \sqrt{\dfrac{\sum x^2 - (\sum x)^2 / n}{n-1}}$, where n is the sample size.

ALL questions should be attempted.

Marks

1. Mary McIntosh works in a knitwear factory.

   For a basic 35-hour week she is paid at the rate of £5·20 per hour and for each jumper she makes over her target of 150, she receives a bonus of £1·35.

   Calculate her gross pay for a week when she makes 200 jumpers.

   3

2. In the diagram opposite AC and BD are arcs of circles with centres at O.

   The radius, OA, is 8 metres and the radius, OB, is 10 metres.

   Angle AOC = 72°.

   Find the shaded area.

   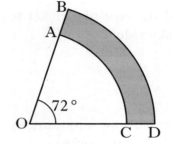

   4

3. The value of a house increased from £85 000 to £86 700 in one year.

   (*a*) What was the percentage increase?

   1

   (*b*) If the value of the house continued to rise at this rate, what would its value be after a **further** 3 years?

   Give your answer to the nearest thousand pounds.

   3

4. A grain store is in the shape of a cylinder with a hemisphere on top as shown in the diagram.

   The cylinder has radius 2·4 metres and height 9·5 metres.

   Find the volume of the grain store.

   Give your answer in cubic metres, correct to 1 significant figure.

   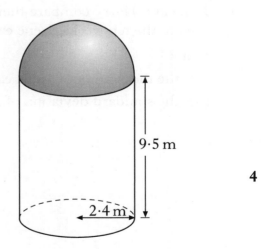

   4

[Turn over

Marks

5. At an amusement park, the Green family buy 3 tickets for the ghost train and 2 tickets for the sky ride. The total cost is £8·60.

    (*a*) Let x pounds be the cost of a ticket for the ghost train and y pounds be the cost of a ticket for the sky ride.

        Write down an equation in x and y which satisfies the above condition.   **1**

    (*b*) The Black family bought 5 tickets for the ghost train and 3 tickets for the sky ride at the same amusement park. The total cost was £13·60.

        Write down a second equation in x and y which satisfies this condition.   **1**

    (*c*) Find the cost of a ticket for the ghost train and the cost of a ticket for the sky ride.   **4**

6. Harry records the amount, in pounds, he earned from his part-time job each week for ten weeks.

        14   18   19   20   17   19   18   20   15   22

He calculates that

$$\sum x = 182 \qquad \text{and} \qquad \sum x^2 = 3364$$

where x is the amount in pounds he earned each week.

    (*a*) Calculate the mean amount he earned per week.   **1**

    (*b*) Using an appropriate formula, calculate the standard deviation.   **2**

    (*c*) Irene and Harry compare their earnings over the ten week period. For each of the ten weeks, Irene earns exactly £5 more than Harry.

        State:

        (i) the mean amount Irene earned per week;   **1**

        (ii) the standard deviation of Irene's earnings.   **1**

Marks

7. A field with sides measuring 12·5 metres, 13·2 metres and 10·7 metres is represented by the triangle PQR shown below.

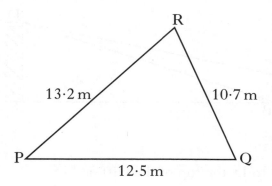

(*a*) Calculate the size of angle PQR.
   Do not use a scale drawing. 3

(*b*) Calculate the area of the field. 2

8. A network is **traversable** if it can be drawn by going over every line once and only once without lifting your pencil.

The network shown opposite
can be traversed by the route:

$A \rightarrow C \rightarrow B \rightarrow A \rightarrow D \rightarrow C \rightarrow E$

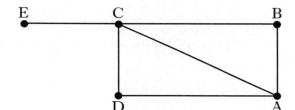

(*a*) Write down a route by which the network below can be traversed.

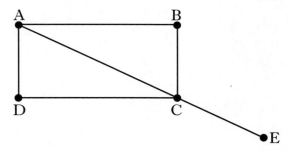

1

(*b*) Write down a route by which the network below can be traversed.

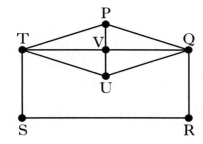

1

Marks

9. To calculate the height of a cliff, a surveyor measures the angle of elevation at two positions A and B as shown in the diagram below.

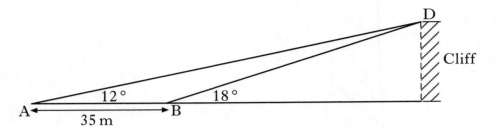

At A, the angle of elevation to D, the top of the cliff, is 12°.

At B, the angle of elevation to D is 18°.

AB is 35 metres.

Calculate the height of the cliff.   **5**

10. (*a*) Multiply out the brackets and collect like terms.

$$(2x + 3)(x^2 - 5x + 2)$$ **3**

(*b*) Factorise

$$2x^2 - 7x - 9.$$ **2**

11. On a spreadsheet, Margaret keeps track of her electricity account for which she receives a statement every two months. She makes a monthly payment towards the cost of the electricity used.

	A	B	C	D	E	F	G
1	**Electricity Account**						
2							
3							
4							
5	**Statements**	**2001**					
6							
7	January–February	£134.68			Monthly payment for 2001	£43.50	
8	March–April	£110.92					
9	May–June	£78.30					
10	July–August	£50.65			**Total paid 2001**		
11	September–October	£64.81					
12	November–December	£104.24					
13							
14	**Total cost for 2001**						
15							
16					**Amount owing**		
17							
18							
19							
20					**Monthly payment for 2002**		
21							
22							

(a) Write down the **formula** for cell B14 to calculate her total annual cost for 2001.   **1**

(b) Margaret chooses to pay £43·50 per month towards the cost of her electricity.

Write down the **formula** for cell F10.   **1**

(c) In cell F16, the formula is

     B14–F10.

Calculate the **amount** that will appear in this cell.   **1**

(d) Margaret estimates that her total payment for the year 2002 will be her total cost for 2001 plus 10%.

For cell F20, write down the **formula** for her estimated monthly payment for 2002.   **2**

[Turn over

Marks

12. An article in a Sunday magazine was analysed to provide a measure of the reading difficulty factor. The number of words in each of the first thirty sentences was recorded.

21	22	28	20	17	8	24	17	17	22
5	21	10	17	25	24	14	36	10	34
28	6	23	31	39	9	8	15	6	14

(*a*) Construct a frequency table with class intervals

    1–5,   6–10,   11–15 etc.   **2**

(*b*) Calculate the mean number of words per sentence.   **4**

[END OF QUESTION PAPER]

INTERMEDIATE 2 2003

X101/202

NATIONAL
QUALIFICATIONS
2003

WEDNESDAY, 21 MAY
1.30 PM – 2.15 PM

MATHEMATICS
INTERMEDIATE 2
Units 1, 2 and
Applications of Mathematics
Paper 1
(Non-calculator)

Read carefully

1   **You may <u>NOT</u> use a calculator.**

2   Full credit will be given only where the solution contains appropriate working.

3   Square-ruled paper is provided.

SCOTTISH
QUALIFICATIONS
AUTHORITY

LIB X101/202 6/3/7970

©

FORMULAE LIST

Sine rule: $\dfrac{a}{\sin A} = \dfrac{b}{\sin B} = \dfrac{c}{\sin C}$

Cosine rule: $a^2 = b^2 + c^2 - 2bc \cos A$ or $\cos A = \dfrac{b^2 + c^2 - a^2}{2bc}$

Area of a triangle: $\text{Area} = \frac{1}{2} ab \sin C$

Volume of a sphere: $\text{Volume} = \frac{4}{3} \pi r^3$

Volume of a cone: $\text{Volume} = \frac{1}{3} \pi r^2 h$

Volume of a cylinder: $\text{Volume} = \pi r^2 h$

Standard deviation: $s = \sqrt{\dfrac{\sum (x - \bar{x})^2}{n-1}} = \sqrt{\dfrac{\sum x^2 - (\sum x)^2 / n}{n-1}}$, where n is the sample size.

ALL questions should be attempted.

Marks

1. Joseph works as a childminder.

   He is paid at a rate of £4·10 per hour for weekdays and at time and a half for weekends.

   One week he works from 9 am till 1 pm every day except Sunday.

   Calculate Joseph's gross pay for that week.

   3

2. Two spinners are used in an experiment.

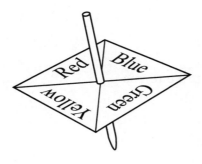 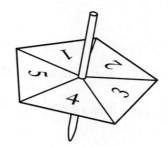

   The table below shows some of the possible outcomes when both spinners are spun and allowed to come to rest.

	1	2	3	4	5
Red	R,1	R,2			
Yellow	Y,1				
Blue	B,1				
Green	G,1				

   (a) Copy and complete the table.

   1

   (b) What is the probability that one spinner comes to rest on red and the other on an even number?

   1

   [Turn over

Marks

3. The diagram shows a cone.

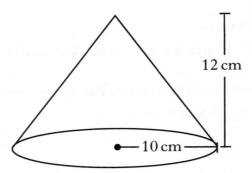

12 cm

10 cm

The height is 12 centimetres and the radius of the base 10 centimetres.
Calculate the volume of the cone.
Take π = 3·14.

2

4. (*a*) Multiply out the brackets and collect like terms.

$$(2a - b)(3a + 2b)$$

2

(*b*) Factorise $7 + 6x - x^2$.

2

Marks

5. A hotel books taxis from a company called QUICKCARS.

The receptionist notes the waiting time for every taxi ordered over a period of two weeks.

The times are recorded in the stem and leaf diagram shown below.

Waiting time (minutes)

```
0 | 6 7
1 | 2 3 4
2 | 5 6 9 9
3 | 2 5 7
4 | 2 4
```

$n = 14$ 1 | 3 represents 13 minutes

(a) For the given data, calculate:
  (i) the median;   1
  (ii) the lower quartile;   1
  (iii) the upper quartile.   1
(b) Calculate the semi-interquartile range.   1

In another two week period, the hotel books taxis from a company called FASTCABS.

The semi-interquartile range for FASTCABS is found to be 2·5 minutes.

(c) Which company provides the more consistent service?

   Give a reason for your answer.   1

6. The diagram below shows part of the London Underground railway network.

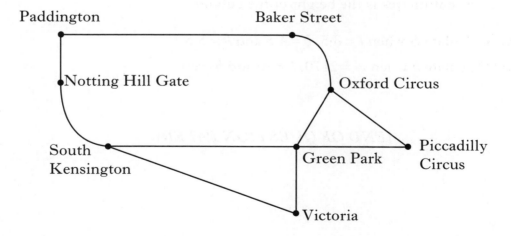

An inspector has to travel along every route shown.

Is it possible to do this without travelling any route more than once?

Explain your answer.   2

[Turn over for Questions 7 and 8 on *Page six*

Marks

7.

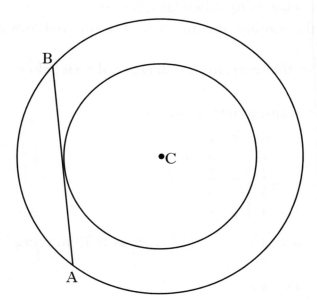

C is the centre of two concentric circles.

AB is a tangent to the smaller circle and a chord of the larger circle.

The radius of the smaller circle is 6 centimetres and the chord AB has length 16 centimetres.

Calculate the radius of the larger circle.

3

8. The surface area, S square centimetres, of a cuboid is given by the formula

$$S = 2lb + 2bh + 2lh$$

where l centimetres is the length of the cuboid
b centimetres is the breadth of the cuboid
h centimetres is the height of the cuboid.

(a) Calculate S when $l = 8 \cdot 5$, $b = 4 \cdot 5$ and $h = 5 \cdot 5$.

2

(b) Calculate h when $S = 2170$, $l = 30$ and $b = 20$.

3

[END OF QUESTION PAPER]

X101/204

NATIONAL
QUALIFICATIONS
2003

WEDNESDAY, 21 MAY
2.35 PM – 4.05 PM

MATHEMATICS
INTERMEDIATE 2
Units 1, 2 and
Applications of Mathematics
Paper 2

Read carefully

1 **Calculators may be used in this paper.**

2 Full credit will be given only where the solution contains appropriate working.

3 Square-ruled paper is provided.

SCOTTISH
QUALIFICATIONS
AUTHORITY

FORMULAE LIST

Sine rule: $\dfrac{a}{\sin A} = \dfrac{b}{\sin B} = \dfrac{c}{\sin C}$

Cosine rule: $a^2 = b^2 + c^2 - 2bc \cos A$ or $\cos A = \dfrac{b^2 + c^2 - a^2}{2bc}$

Area of a triangle: $\text{Area} = \frac{1}{2}ab \sin C$

Volume of a sphere: $\text{Volume} = \frac{4}{3}\pi r^3$

Volume of a cone: $\text{Volume} = \frac{1}{3}\pi r^2 h$

Volume of a cylinder: $\text{Volume} = \pi r^2 h$

Standard deviation: $s = \sqrt{\dfrac{\sum(x - \bar{x})^2}{n-1}} = \sqrt{\dfrac{\sum x^2 - (\sum x)^2 / n}{n-1}}$, where n is the sample size.

ALL questions should be attempted.

Marks

1.

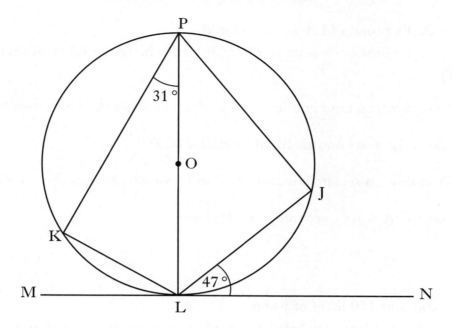

The tangent, MN, touches the circle, centre O, at L.

Angle JLN = 47°.

Angle KPL = 31°.

Find the size of angle KLJ.

3

2. A sample of shoppers was asked which brand of washing powder they preferred.

The responses are shown below.

Washing Powder	Frequency
Dazzle	250
Cyclo	375
Surfer	125
Cleano	250

Construct a pie chart to illustrate this information.

Show all your working.

3

[Turn over

Marks

3. Seats on flights from London to Edinburgh are sold at two prices, £30 and £50.

   On one flight a total of 130 seats was sold.

   Let x be the number of seats sold at £30 and y be the number of seats sold at £50.

   (a) Write down an equation in x and y which satisfies the above condition.   **1**

   The sale of the seats on this flight totalled £6000.

   (b) Write down a second equation in x and y which satisfies this condition.   **1**

   (c) How many seats were sold at each price?   **4**

4. A bath contains 150 litres of water.

   Water is drained from the bath at a steady rate of 30 litres per minute.

   The graph of the volume, V litres, of water in the bath against the time, t minutes, is shown below.

   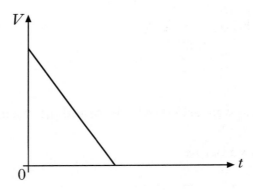

   Write down an equation connecting V and t.   **3**

Marks

5. A gardener grows tomatoes in his greenhouse.

The temperature of the greenhouse, in degrees Celsius, is recorded every day at noon for one week.

17   22   25   16   21   16   16

(a) For the given temperatures, calculate:

(i) the mean;   1

(ii) the standard deviation.   3

Show clearly all your working.

For best growth, the mean temperature should be $(20 \pm 5)°C$ and the standard deviation should be less than $5°C$.

(b) Are the conditions in the greenhouse likely to result in best growth?

Explain clearly your answer.   2

[Turn over

6. A garden trough is in the shape of a prism.

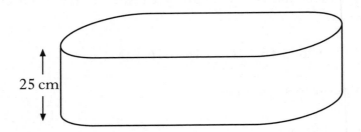

The height of the trough is 25 centimetres.

The cross-section of the trough consists of a rectangle and two semi-circles with measurements as shown.

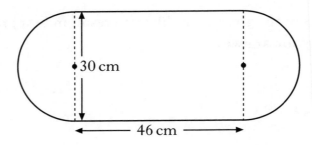

(a) Find the volume of the garden trough in cubic centimetres.

Give your answer correct to two significant figures. **4**

A new design of garden trough is planned by the manufacturer.

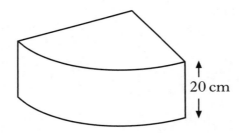

The height of the trough is 20 cm.

The uniform cross-section of this trough is a quarter of a circle.

The volume of the trough is $30\,000\,\text{cm}^3$.

(b) Find the radius of the cross-section. **3**

Marks

7. Ali is paid a basic annual salary plus commission on his sales as shown in the table below.

Sales	Rate of commission on Sales
Less than £25 000	1·5%
£25 000 to £50 000	1·75%
More than £50 000	2·0%

His basic annual salary is **£8500**.

(a) If he achieves sales of £24 900, what will his total annual salary be? **2**

(b) What would Ali's sales need to be to achieve a total annual salary of £9600? **4**

8. The diagram below shows a big wheel at a fairground.

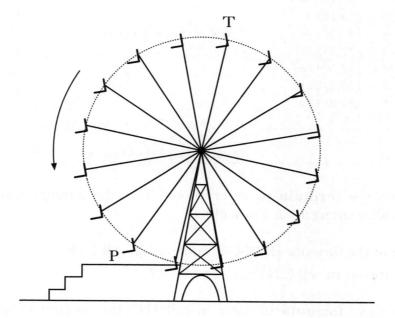

The wheel has sixteen chairs equally spaced on its circumference.

The radius of the wheel is 9 metres.

As the wheel rotates in an anticlockwise direction, find the distance a chair travels in moving from position T to position P in the diagram. **4**

[Turn over

Marks

9. Irum needs a mortgage of £54 500 and wants to make payments of £500 per month.

   She designs a spreadsheet to compare the costs of two mortgages.

   Solid Homes Building Society calculates the interest each month (0·52% per month).

   Evergreen Building Society calculates the interest each year (6·4% per annum).

	A	B	C	D	E	F	G	H
1	Solid Homes Building Society				Evergreen Building Society			
2								
3	Interest charged	0.52% per month			Interest charged	6.4% per annum		
4								
5	Amount owed		£54,500		Amount owed			£54,500
6	Monthly payment		£500		Monthly payment			£500
7								
8	Amount owed	after interest	after payment					
9								
10	January	£54,783.40	£54,283.40		Amount owed at start of year			£54,500
11	February	£54,565.67	£54,065.67					
12	March	£54,346.82	£53,846.82		Annual interest			
13	April	£54,126.82	£53,626.82					
14	May	£53,905.68	£53,405.68					
15	June	£53,683.39	£53,183.39					
16	July	£53,459.94	£52,959.94		Total payments for year			£6,000
17	August	£53,235.33	£52,735.33					
18	September	£53,009.56	£52,509.56					
19	October	£52,782.61	£52,282.61					
20	November	£52,554.48	£52,054.48					
21	December							
22								
23	Amount owed at end of year				Amount owed at end of year			

(a) Write down the **formula** to enter in cell B21 the amount owed in December after interest has been added. 1

(b) The result of the formula =B21−C6 is entered in cell C21.
   What will appear in cell C21? 1

(c) Write down the **formula** to enter in cell H12 the amount of annual interest. 1

(d) Which mortgage is more expensive in the first year, and by how much? 2

Marks

10. The sketch shows a parallelogram, PQRS.

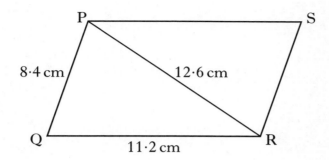

(a) Calculate the size of angle PQR.

Do not use a scale drawing.   3

(b) Calculate the area of the parallelogram.   3

11. A survey was carried out to find the average price of a washing machine. The results are shown in the table below.

Price	Frequency	Cumulative frequency
251–300	8	
301–350	12	
351–400	18	
401–450	25	
451–500	19	
501–550	10	
551–600	6	
601–650	2	

(a) Copy and complete the table.   1

(b) Using this data, draw a cumulative frequency curve on squared paper.   3

(c) From the curve you have drawn, estimate the median price of the washing machines.   1

[END OF QUESTION PAPER]